Contents

Introduction

Hello and welcome to our book on Psychology of Personality. The aim of the book is to gain in-depth knowledge of the psychology of the personality, to understand why this part of psychological science is important, and how generally personal psychology contributes to the behaviour and life of the person. The book is divided into five main topics into the most influential theoretical concepts and schools on understanding the notion of personality.

First, we will introduce you the psychoanalytic personality theory created by Sigmund Freud. We will turn our attention to the three psychic structures (Id, Ego and the Super-ego), their functions and meaning. We will look at the notion of a person in terms of classical psychoanalysis. We will introduce you Freud's ideas and views on the Life Drive and the Death Drive.

Second, we will present you the ideas and views of Karl Gustav Jung and analytical psychology about the personality. We will focus on some differences in Jung and Freud's views and we will look at the three personality structures in the theory of Jung. We will introduce you the idea of the personal consciousness, personal unconscious and the collective unconscious, their meaning and functions, and we will look at the typology of the personality created by Jung, which most people know as the psychological concepts "introvert" and "extravert".

Third, we will present you the ideas and views of Erich Fromm and his critique of Sigmund Freud's theories. We'll look at the escape mechanisms dealt with by Fromm. We will focus on Karen Horney's insight into the female psyche and her views on anxiety, and we will look at the personal orientations described by her.

Fourth, we will present you the ideas and views of Alfred Adler and the individual psychology. We will look at his social approach to the personality. We will look at the social interest, its significance and its functions. We will introduce you Adler's idea of the feeling of inferiority and the inferiority complex and how it can be overcome. And we will introduce you the hypothesis raised by Adler about the leader of our lives, namely the sense of authority and superiority.

Fifth, we will present you the situational and the dispositional approach to the personality. We will look at the ideas and views of Gordon Allport, Hans Eysenck, Kurt Lewin, Raymond Bernard Cattell and Walter Mischel. We will introduce the idea of features and dispositions. We will also look at the main criticisms of the two approaches to explaining the person.

What you'll learn?

1. What is personality?

2. What are the ideas and views of Sigmund Freud and the Classic Psychoanalytic Theory about the personality.

3. What are the ideas and views of Karl Gustav Jung and the Analytic Psychology Theory about the personality.

4. What are the ideas and views of Erich Fromm, Karen Horney and the Neo-Freudian theories about the personality.

5. What are the ideas and views of Alfred Adler and the Individual-Psychological Theory about Personality.

6. What are the ideas and views of Gordon Allport, Hans Eysenck, Kurt Lewin, Raymond Bernard Cattell and Walter Mischel and the situational and the dispositional method of approach to the personality.

For whom is this book for?

1. Psychologists
2. Psychiatrist
3. Teachers
4. Pedagogues
5. Social Workers
6. Medical Practitioners
7. Nurses
8. Parents
9. Academicians
10. Students
11. Anyone Who Is Interested In: Personality Psychology

WHY THIS BOOK AND TOPIC ARE SO IMPORTANT?

In our dynamic everyday life, everyone faces people with different and unique personal psychology. This book is important and useful because we have based it solely on the scientific information we have presented in an easy and accessible way. The better we know ourselves and our personal psychology, and the individual psychology of others, the better we will understand where our differences and our similarities arise and so we could live, communicate and coexist together. We have adhered to the idea of not making the book unnecessarily long, filled with irrelevant and useless information. Everything you find in it can be applied directly to your daily life in one way or another without much effort, cost and time.

ABOUT THE AUTHOR

 Valentin Boyadzhiev is a trained nutritionist, graduated Master of Psychology in "Psychology and Psychopathology of Development". He has acquired Professional Qualification "Teacher of Psychology" and Postgraduate Professional Qualification "Psychological Counseling in Psychosomatic and Social Adaptation Disorders". He has obtained a Psychoanalysis Diploma and he is currently specializing in Psychoanalytic Psychotherapy. He is a member of the Association "Bulgarian Psychoanalytic Space", "International Society of Applied Psychoanalysis" and „International Alliance of Holistic Therapists". He is a lecturer on issues related to nutrition, diet, supplementation, food and sports. He is also a teacher and a lecturer in the field of psychology, logic, ethics, law, and philosophy. He has been a school psychologist since 2017. He has been participating annually in scientific conferences on psychology, psychotherapy, dietetics and medicine. His main interest and practice are in the field of psychoanalysis and clinical psychology. For more information about the autor, you can check out his official website www.valentinboyadzhiev.com. The working language of

the site is Bulgarian, but you can easily translate it.

SPECIAL THANKS

I would like to express my special thanks to Glory Dimitrova, without whose help this book would not be a fact. She was the person who put a great deal of effort and dedication in the translation of the text and its proper layout. Also, she has a Master Degree in Law and always strives to present our e-books, video certification courses and other activities in the best and most accessible way to a wide audience of interested people.

Psychoanalytic Personality Theory. Ideas and Views of Sigmund Freud.

Strictly speaking, this is the first personality theory created by Sigmund Freud in the twenties of the 20th century. On this theory and its possibilities are written thousands of pages of admiration and criticism, but as one says "despite the harsh criticism already 100 so and more years it does not leave the scene of psychological science because it deals with issues which have a stunning burden for our lives, for the reason that this theory has social, moral, ethical, anthropological resonance on an understanding of human nature". There is no psychological theory that is not based on a certain point of view for man. Usually, there is a meeting of biological and cultural-historical approaches, and from here unfinished discussions and controversies begin. In Freud's concept of personality, there is something unique about the fact that this theory is built on the dialectics of conscious and unconscious psyche. Dialectics is a science of the fact that the phenomena are contradictory. When something new appears, it contains something old. Such an understanding and view where the presence of the unconscious psychic in the soul of man shocks humanity. Shocking is that Sigmund Freud creates another image of man. He says, "You are not really what you think that you are", "You are not masters in your own home". He thinks that human behaviour is guided by motifs we do not realize, but in their place, we put reasonable explanations. Freud was the first to characterize the psyche as a battlefield between the irreconcilable forces of drives and reason, nature and culture, the biological and social. Until the 20s of the 20th Century, he affirms the view that man is the bearer of a conscious and unconscious psyche. After 1920, he is taking a step forward and building a psyche structure. This structure allows the theory to be called "psychoanalytic" or "depth" or "confrontational". In a sense, it is "motivational," and the common name of this theory and the theories that resemble it is "psychoanalytic". The term "dynamic" replaces the term "change". This term describes the change of structures and the interaction between them. According to psychoanalysis, the life of a person is accompanied by an inner conflict that is based on unconscious, primary, sexual, and aggressive tendencies.

What is personality?

According to Sigmund Freud, the personality is a psychodynamic structure of processes in a state of conflict which regulates behaviour. Freud creates the idea of the three structural psychic instances (Id, Ego and Super-ego).

But what is hiding behind them?

Id is the unconscious part of the psyche or the psychic apparatus (this part appears before the consciousness). Id contains everything inherited and repressed which is unconscious. This psychic instance/structure is not a reflection of the outside world, its core is the instinct or more specifically - the drive. Works on "the pleasure principle". He also thinks that people are born with primary drives and that there is a hierarchy of these drives. He also raises the hypothesis that the main tendency of the unconscious is satisfaction, which in turn is accompanied by a pleasant experience, and exactly because of that there is no morality, since experiencing pleasure is a natural pursuit and cannot be condemned. Morality could be found in the manner in which we get satisfaction and this manner is designed by the culture.

Somewhere higher and later the consciousness appears. This part of the psyche Freud marks by the name **"Ego"**. In his view, consciousness evolvingly arises as a structure and process. Its occurrence is related to servicing the unconscious, searching for objects to satisfy the drives and the needs. Consciousness works on the "reality principle" which means one knows the outside world, the time, the space, and only in the sense of consciousness one can distinguish the real from the fantasmic object. Ego acquires a role and a value when it becomes clear that it is capable of internalizing/assuming cultural rules and norms, exercising control and resistance against the catharsis and the pressure of the drives, to work as something more which is above the Ego called "Super-ego".

The **Super-ego**, in its content, is not a biological structure. It is content acquired from culture, first through the parents, then through the school and the requirements of the institutions. Sigmund Freud, calls this structure conscience or censorship. **What does Super-ego do?** It guides, forbids, allows, controls, and all of this is in the form of our consent. If we manifest incompatible behaviour with the Super-ego, we experience a sense of guilt, but if we do not accept certain requirements, we do not feel guilty. **What lies behind the guilt?** The answer is clear - the fear of being rejected by others. When there are fantasmic ideas in the Super-ego that eliminate the value of the other, the justice, and when a morality that overlooks others is respected, this Super-ego acts as a pathology. It is not difficult to find a person with a hypertrophic Super-ego. The hypertrophic Super-ego always reduces the value of the Ego and can crush it and depersonalize it. The Super-ego functions as a social unconscious. There are also people with a very developed/ autonomous Ego.

The three structures Id - Ego - Super-ego have a complex internal dynamics, and according to Sigmund Freud, the early years of human life (up to the age of 5-7) and the events that occurred during these years are crucial to the development and formation of the personality. During these years there may be different clashes, traumas and failures in development. Freud believes in the so-called biographical/event factor. It is the idea that the character is formed depending on what happened to the individual. If at a certain stage the drive doesn't receive satisfaction, the individual will be afraid to go to a higher stage, and thus a fixation is obtained at that stage, and if he receives a flawless and endless satisfaction, he will not want to move further and he will have a fixation on the stage of the satisfaction. If there is a fixation, then at later stages of development, the individual will want this satisfaction that he had at the earlier stage. If an individual is fixated in the oral stage but is already an adult, he can seek satisfaction in drinking, eating and smoking. Such a late fixation accompanied by a return to that passed, but satisfying stage is called regression. Regression is an individual's striving to live in a way that is experienced at an earlier stage. Regression occurs when there is a lot of stress in the later stages. The peculiarities arose out of the early stages appeared in the later stages of personality development.

Stages of development as a tool for typology of personality:

Oral personality - Here the main area of excitement is the mouth. Middle-aged people who are fixated at this stage have an orality that occurs in eating, smoking, kissing. There is harmony between sexual and aggressive tendencies. They are primarily interested in themselves. They are a narcissistic type of persons. Other people acquire meaning for them through what they give. Oral persons are a receiving types of people. They are "cultural beggars". They possess disguised aggression. They are demanding, jealous, impatient, vindictive, pessimistic, suppressed, "if they suck, they won't let go".

Anal Personality - Here the satisfaction of needs and drive is related to the anal appeal. Learning to go to the toilet is a socio-psychic process and it reflects the authority of the parent and the way this authority is used. The middle-aged person who is fixated at this stage is a very cold, peculiar type. He is relieving himself from all the inconveniences, from everything bad. When he does it, he is satisfied, not shamed. He is rigid, firm, impermeable. He possesses a sense of power and control over others. He has a strong interest in how he looks and how he behaves. The main fear of this type of personality is the "fear of losing control." He enjoys the pleasure of acquiring a property. The anxiety of this type of personality is between the two forms of evolutionary reactions "to fight" and "to obey". The transition from oral to anal personality develops from the "give me" position to "do what I say". It can be assumed that this personality is an illustration of the contradiction - release from the inside and demands from the outside.

Phallic personality - This stage is characterized and centred on sexual and aggressive feelings associated with sexual organs and erogenous zones. It is assumed that there is a bit of identification with the Oedipus complex. The fixation is different for men and women. The man rejects the possibility of castration ("I am great in the eyes of others"). At this stage, the woman identifies herself with her mother. The woman is hysterical (romanticizes life and relationship with the man). Castration anxiety pushes the sexual desire towards the mother and enhances the hatred to the father. The Super-ego, in turn, is the heir of the Oedipus complex and blocks/inhibits the movement towards incest and aggression. Rediscovery of childhood and fixation in later ages is a natural content of the psychoanalytic method. The fixations are related to serious work with the Ego and the Super-ego.

After 1921/1922 Sigmund Freud came to the conclusion that human functioning had a motive. This motive he sees in the face of the two main tendencies or drives: The first is the so-called "Life Drive". It is characterized by the fact that it preserves and proceeds life. It is a constructive and creative drive. Freud calls him "Eros". The second is the so-called "Death Drive". It is characterized by its destruction, aggression and mortification. It is a necrophilia drive. This is where the many disagreements with Sigmund Freud's theory begin, which will be discussed in the following lectures.

He announces that the drives are the main content of human motivation, calling them "obsessive motives". You can not reverse, forbid or avoid them. The tendency towards death creates the bad image of man. Sigmund Freud is a representative of the solid Jewish thought, which means that he is a dialectician. He says that the contradictory in the face of opposites is the fundamental property of being. Every thing has its opposite. There is creation, but there is also destruction. Life is a backward movement to death. He is also a representative of Ernst Haeckel's old German physicochemical school, which says that individual development of man is an abbreviated repetition of the phylogenetic development of humanity. Freud witnesses the First World War and asks, "What is the cause of this destruction?". These illogical, destructive phenomena in life make him allow such a basic inclination, namely, "Death Drive". He thinks that mankind cannot overcome its destructive attraction. He thinks that in the flow of our lives, the sexual drive or the so-called "Life Drive" is stronger and significantly blocks the pressure of the aggressive drive "Death Drive". People have an affection to life and partly controls their aggressive drive. Freud discovers the fact that sexual instinct suffers deformities not for biological reasons but for cultural and historical situations. It is true that this instinct maintains the type of homo sapiens. In the sexual act, which is one of the drive's realizations, two tendencies, two impulses, two needs, two inclinations meet. On one side is the sexuality that has a biological origin, and on the other is the socio-cultural directions, that is the model of the realization of sexuality, the choice of partner, etc. There are cultural norms that are needed, but there are ones that deform sexual drive. Freud thinks that the problem of pleasure is that there is more to one, and to others less, and concludes that human life is flowing into the conflict between instinct and culture that is initially hostile to the drive. Freud says that by virtue of this conflict, in this functioning is involved "Ego", that is, the face of our consciousness.

As a conclusion to this lecture, we will say that the building of psychoanalysis is not built only from clinical cases but from a forest of reliable observations, which, according to Sigmund Freud, are stronger than any experiment. Freud accepts the stories of his patients for scientific data. Everyone can imagine what a great method is the introspection of the couch, free from all limitations and inhibitions. The analytical séance is a scientific method more valuable than the experiment because it is unique in necessity, it is a natural experiment. There are no artefacts, no experience of something that is not in life. Psychoanalysis is defended as a science by the success it achieves.

Analytical Theory of Personality. Ideas and Views of Carl Gustav Jung.

Carl Gustav Jung's figure and work are often put on the same level as Freud's. Jung's family comes from Germany, he is a doctor and a psychologist, and his life is flowing in Basil. The portrait created by Sigmund Freud is subject to criticism, disagreement and contradictory assessments, including by his followers and students. The most critical and dramatic is the conflict with Carl Gustav Jung. The year of the critical conflict is 1913.

Karl Gustav Jung has a different idea and point of view on the source and causes of neuroses. According to Freud, the source is the childhood traumas, but according to Jung there are many factors such as misfortune in life, unhealthy human relationships, work failures, and life as a whole, and of course, it does not exclude factors of a sexual nature. Jung does not accept the Oedipus complex by believing that parents are not sexual but moral partners of the child. He does not accept the concept of "sexual energy". They have a different technique of performing of the seances in particular patient-client physical contact. Freud does not allow it. They also do not share the same view on the interpretation of dreams. But these differences are not the main reason for the separation between them. The big reason is rooted in the different perspectives on the structure of the psyche and the understanding of the nature of the unconscious. For Jung, the psyche is the equivalent of the personality. And this is the reason why two different theories of personality arise.

Jung has ideas on the archetypal appearance of the personality. He talks about "persona" - the mask of the actors with which they play a certain role. He thinks we have an archetype, an unconscious and conscious predisposition to behave in a certain way in different situations and relationships. Personality is understood as a "persona" with the mask that a person puts in to present himself in a particular way that he desires in front of others. He shows an "external personality," and if he becomes obsessed with that personality he becomes a sick person. The point of view of the personality as a "persona" says and suggests a fundamental and undeniable fact that people are personalities when they are adequate to the situation in which they function. The archetypal notion of personality orients towards a perception of personality associated with an adequate human change in a given situation.

Jung talks about the three personality structures:

Personal consciousness - this concept is related to the analysis of the main functions of consciousness such as sensation, thinking, intuition and feelings. This notion describes the man as the holder of conscious functions.

The personal unconscious - this concept refers to the unconscious contents related to the events of the individual life, the personal experience that we have accumulated and pushed/repressed. The personal unconscious is similar in character to the Freud's repressed unconscious, but with a peculiarity, Jung announces that the core of the personal unconscious is "the complex". The complexes are pushed/repressed emotionally saturated contents, complicating our adaptive behaviour.

Collective/universal/generic unconscious - this idea and hypothesis is a central point in the psychological portrayal of the personality and marks the fundamental difference between Sigmund Freud and Carl Gustav Jung regarding the main principle of the psyche. Jung brings out the functioning of psyche from cultural, racial factors with a social nature related to the subject's attitude towards the objects, unlike Sigmund Freud, who brings the functioning of the psyche out of biological factors. Jung believes that in the structure of the human psyche there is a layer, space and judgment that is deepest in the cave, where the experience of all mankind, people of all ages, races, and cultures is postponed, to start with something clear - an experience of how to react, an experience that does not represent knowledge. Collective unconscious is content that is not conscious but influences thoughts, feelings, ideas, and actions. It structures the psyche and behaviour. The collective unconscious is an experience but in a particular form. It is an inherited experience at the neural level of responding in a certain way to significant and recurrent events and objects in our lives. The way of reaction is accomplished as a predisposition, as an instruction we do not realize, as a rule without content, which we apply to the actual content. The collective unconscious has a constructive character in terms of the objective world. These non-content rules correlated and specified to certain objects are called archetypes. These archetypes are revealed in symbols. Archetypal symbols are symbols of the unconscious and are different from the symbols of consciousness.

Jung has explored such archetypes as:
• The most important for of the personality are the "persona", the Ego, the shadow;
• The mother;
• The anima and the animus;
• The deities and others.

Jung also makes one of the early typologies of the personality. His typology refers to healthy people but can be used and applied to the sick. These are the phenomena of "extraversion" and "introversion". He assumes that the lives of some people are dependent and determined more by the connection with external objects, and the lives of others - more than the connection with their own experiences and life. Therefore, people have an interaction with two worlds - both external and internal, but each person prefers one of them. The introvert disregards himself from objects, seeks freedom from the outside world, and reduces its significance to its own existence. Jung says: "The standard introvert is characterized by fluctuating reflexivity and endangered nature which is seeking solitary. The introvert preserves himself because of himself. He retires from the objects and always remains in some defensive position". The extravert is outwardly oriented. Accepts objects positively. He strives to discover and increase their value. Jung says, "Extraversion is characterized by mobility, open-heartedness, conciliatoriness, living nature, easy adaptability, easily create connections and affection. In the extravert attitude dominates the external factor". The subject-to-object relation is always a matter of adaptation. Jung says, "It's a fundamental contrast that sometimes turns out to be brighter, sometimes blurred, but always to people with a prominent personality. Extravert and Introvert types are not affected by gender, education, environment, or heredity. They are influenced by the convenience of adaptation". Jung also shows that the functions of the personal consciousness acquires particularities depending on whether we are extraverts or introverts. These two orientations/characteristics such as name and content are used in other theories, mostly dispositions, and their content is expanded. This is based on the clusterization of qualities to a level of generalization.

Jung also develops the associative experiment - this method is projective and has unlimited possibilities as long as one knows what to subordinate to. Associative experiments attack the individuality of a person!

A careful look at psychoanalytic theories shows that they give a significant place to the personality as modelled by the unconscious psyche. But this is not all, these theories provoke questions such as "How conscious is a man and how conscious he is not?" and also questions are raised such as "What place has the particular culture, the social and economic structure of society for to the formation of the person?"

As a conclusion, we will quote Jung's words: "She (psychology) is still in the cradle, and so the time of the generalizing theories has not yet occurred. Even sometimes it seems to me, that psychology has not understood either the scale of its tasks or the confusing and complex nature of its subject - the psyche itself". According to him, her subject matter is maddening!

Neo-Freudian theories of personality. The Ideas and Views of Erich Fromm and Karen Horney.

The first correction of psychoanalytic theories can be found in neo-Freudians' views, particularly in the views of Erich Fromm, Karen Horney and Harry Sullivan.

Erich Fromm appears on the stage as the founder of a system of views that hit the critical points of the personality. Fromm sociologizes (interprets from a sociological point of view) the psychoanalytic view to man and emphasizes the fact that people are the product of inevitable human relationships. In the formation of the theory of personality, Fromm makes a clash between the cultural and the biological and says that our biological assets must adapt to culture and society. **What is the nature of man?** Nature is the starting point from which personality is defined. To define the nature of man, Erich Fromm gives a meeting of Sigmund Freud and Karl Marx as a non-partisan reading of Marx and says: "Marx has studied the outside nature of the human being, the dependence of man on other people, that is, the dictatorship of society over man, Freud has studied the dependence that comes from within, from the drive. By virtue of this dependence man has a dualistic nature". At the same time, Erich Fromm has a firm social view of the essence of man. Contextually, Erich Fromm reaffirms the idea that personality is the essence of man, that the personality is social and is the connection with the other people. If the essence of the personality is the relationships with other people, then the question arises what the others give to the personality and what the individual give them and how they function as personalities. Every society has created certain economic, political and legal rules of life. Erich Fromm analyzes the life of man from the Middle Ages to the present day, and establishes that for centuries, man has become more and freer, but this freedom has a price - he is losing more and more security for his life. "The only living thing that turns his own existence into a problem is a man." By gaining freedom, but losing security, a person runs away from freedom and seeks a way to find and gain security. Erich Fromm described brilliantly this aspect of the personality through the escape mechanisms:

Authoritarianism, that is, the attempt to join with something that you agree to and obtain security and even power.
Obedience, that is, trying to find security through the obedience of another person. There are also many unconscious motives.
Conformity, that is, trying to find security by changing your own point of view under the pressure of the group.

Fromm concludes that man is lonely and alienated and is under the sign of overcoming this loneliness and alienation. Erich Fromm's views on man and personality are an appeal to a change in the nature of man. He says change can occur when there is a fair, social, economic and moral society, and aggression is caused by the fact that the problems are not solved in the same way for all.

Karen Horney is deeply acquainted with Freudism, a practitioner doctor, a psychotherapist, and a solid theoretical scientist. She takes a look at the personality by analyzing the phenomenon and the concept of **"anxiety"** and, in a sense, by analyzing the concept of "female psyche". She creates a simple, understandable, trustworthy personality orientation of anxiety-related people by defining **three types of personalities** that every psychotherapist works without even knowing. The main concept in Horney's theory of personality is the notion of **"basal anxiety"**. Anxiety is one of the phenomena in the structure of the psyche. Eventually, people are divided into calm and worried/anxious. Anxiety is a state in which a person experiences himself as useless, scared of life/being, despising himself, hostile to others and the world as self-denying. Roughly speaking, here thinking is distorted, in principle rejecting. The anxious person has a need to connect with other people, from love, recognition, independence, and coping with problems. The anxious people carry low self-esteem and, in this sense, this is not adequate. There is also a fixation on how they see other people. Karen Horney has a definite advantage in understanding this phenomenon. She makes a psychographic/psychobiographical analysis of anxiety and starts from the fact that young children experience their connection with their parents as physical and mental dependence. If a child lives in a normal atmosphere, a little major but not hysterical, things are fine. If, however, the atmosphere is unhealthy, traumatic - the child is experiencing himself/herself as frightened, vulnerable. Here, says Horney, basal anxiety appears. The child experiences himself/herself a discarded, useless, gotten into an irrational world. The rejected person, the rejected child is anxious, hates his parents, but is weak and can not punish them. Anxicty is an cxperience, a state and a trait that shapes every expression of a person.

Anxiety is a consequence of:
1. Alienation by parents;
2. Lack of parents;
3. Excessive control;
4. A hostile atmosphere in which the child lives (maltreatment, beating);
5. Discrimination/neglect especially in the conditions of several children;
6. A great admiration directed at the child;
7. Excessive love for the child;

There is physiological anxiety associated with the physiological needs associated with whether they are satisfied or not and the psychic anxiety that arises in relation to the adequacy of the Ego-image. There is a difference in knowing who you are in relation to the attitude towards this knowledge. In some people this is adequate and critical, in others it is inadequate and uncritical.

What personal orientations are observed?

Compliant personality - Orientation Towards People - the behaviour of this type of personality is characterized by indecision, helplessness and dependence. This type says, "Ah, how poor and unhappy I am." A person is aware of the need for a partner, friend, spouse, guide, beloved, or relationship. The pursuit of this strategy aims to reduce tension, to reach safety and security. The slogan of these people is, "If I comply, they will not disturb me, they will not bother me." The compliant person mentally wants to be loved, accepted, protected and guided, to be necessary, not isolated. This is a survival strategy, and here is often discussed whether there is no hidden masochism and whether behind this culturally justified servility is hidden concealed aggression. This personality has low self-esteem, plays the role of being weak and unhappy. Sexual acts are passive. Here is a manifestation of the evolutionary reaction **obedience**.

Aggressive Personality - Orientation Against People - The slogan of this type of personality is "I have power, no one can push me. Life is a struggle of everyone against everyone. What is important is what I get - money, power, love, idea, it does not matter." This type of personality acts tactical and amicable in the name of the benefit (utilitarian types). Narcissistic, in love with himself, idealizes his image. Haughty, vengeful, proud, strong, leader and guide. Perfectionist, oriented to high standards he chooses the best if he is the one who chooses. The needs of this type of personality are to be the first, to always win, to have a reputation, to be respected and accepted. These people are instrumental, users, they use the others. The main orientation of this type is power over the surroundings. Here is a manifestation of the evolutionary **battle** reaction.

Withdrawing personality - Orientation From People - the attitude of this type of personality is "I do not care; if I exclude myself and if I suspend myself, everything will be fine." Here acts the evolutionary regimes and **escaping** reactions. These people do not invest themselves. They are relieved of involvement. They are self-sufficient. They discover everything in themselves. They move in indifferently and evenly, superficially, have no affinity for emotional experiences. They are focused on solitude and do not solve basal anxiety through power or love. They protect their own private life. Many withdrawing types are artists and their isolation is a comfortable condition. The main tendency is that they seek and discover everything in themselves.

All three strategies are aimed at reducing the sense of anxiety that arises from social relationships. The healthy person, unlike the neurotic, uses all three strategies, combines them and adapts successfully. The neurotic one works with one of the strategies, fixes on it, and treats negatively the other strategies.

Individual-Psychological Theory of Personality. The Ideas and Views of Alfred Adler.

Alfred Adler is a member of Freud's Vienna circle and IPA (International Psychoanalysis Association). He is an Austrian doctor and psychologist with high social and civic culture and independence. In 1911, he expressed views other than those of Sigmund Freud and, together with eight other people, the "gang of the ninth" was excluded from the psychoanalytic movement. He takes a standalone path of development and sets the foundations for a movement called individual psychology. His views are particularly related to his personal life. He has a traumatic childhood and a later life like this. One morning he finds his brother with whom they are sleeping in the same bed dead. He experiences heavily and suffers a lot because of his qualification of a mentally retarded person when he was in the first grade. Adler graduated excellently medicine at the University of Vienna. In 1920 there was a refusal of having the academical rank to be a professor at the University of Vienna. He graduated in medicine, having at first practice as an ophthalmologist, then as a psychologist.

The disagreement with Sigmund Freud is actually a difference in the main motive of human life. Sigmund Freud puts the sexual motives first, while Adler puts the social interest, where the main purpose of life is to acquire status, a position of value among other people, articulated as a sense of power and superiority. He raises the slogan "Man has something more than heredity and the environment. He has an artistic or a creative Ego", which means that he can create himself. The requirements of the environment and human activity develop the person. Alfred Adler is an early harbinger of humanistic psychology. Indivisible, holistic, but he looks at life and concludes and says there are no perfect people. According to him, people have problems, defects, shortcomings. People have a sense of inferiority or inability since their childhood. This feeling makes us struggle, make efforts, compensate and overcome the incompleteness. Occasionally, the opposite is the case, a person is making efforts but does not succeed. He may attach an explanatory role to some defect or fault, fix himself on the defect, and obtain an inferiority complex. The complex is something that tortures people. The term was introduced by Carl Gustav Jung. The complex is an experience grouped around an object to which we have a negative feeling. According to Adler, if a person is loved, he gets security from other people, if he is acknowledged, respected if he is valuable to others if he has his own environment for which he is important, he doesn't posses complexes. In his view, the overcoming of these complexes and the acquisition of a sense of authority and superiority make us healthy people.

It is important to understand that Adler does not understand superiority as leadership, power, wealth, for him superiority is upward movement, growth, gaining importance, it is the "great movement upward". He thinks this feeling is innate. Energy is drawn from the desire to raise. In his look at the person, Adler applies the concept of lifestyle or vital style. Every person has his/her individual line of development, an individual way to interact with the world and with himself/herself. Vital style fixates the uniqueness of a person. It also builds the biography of a person. He believes that the explanations for the formation of human character are very naive.

What does human character do?

Adler thinks that the most important factor in the formation of human character is a person's biography. Events form the attitude of a person. Personality cannot be seen outside the gained experience. According to Adler, the lifestyle does not have a common pattern of development and is driven by the ultimate goal. The goal is achieved individually, it is formed too early and in the course of life, people can be aware of their defects and compensate them and change them.

Alfred Adler is a figure in the analytical movement that deserves attention not only because he takes a step to the left of Sigmund Freud, but first of all because his point of view for people has original dimensions, both for his time and today. It is also an example of how the personal life of a human, the experience he has acquired can influence the views for the personality. In 1910-1911, he expressed points of view that did not agree with those of Sigmund Freud. In his general orientation towards the person, he realizes a social approach. While Sigmund Freud claims that the main motive is sexual interest, Alfred Adler argues that the main motive that guides and structures the lifestyle together with the ultimate goal is the social interest, that is, a person in his life strives to achieve a status of value, significance, of acceptance by other people, the status of which the other name is a sense of authority and superiority.

As a citizen and physician Alfred Adler fixates on the obvious fact that there are no perfect people. People have problems, defects, flaws, inconsistencies, and in practice, since childhood, each of us is incomplete. Everyone has a sense and consciousness of inferiority, and the desired status of significance makes him struggle, overcome the difficulties and himself and grow. These efforts make sense because Alfred Adler says: "Everyone has the potential for development and a mechanism to develop these potentials. We have more than heredity and the environment. We have a creative self, we can create ourselves, we can cope with the sense of inferiority with its defects. "It may happen that one could fail, doesn't have luck and then asks himself: "Why?" It can attribute an explanatory value to its defect. When the defect begins to torment us, to possess us, to negatively influence the self, the feeling of inferiority has already been transformed into an inferiority complex. The complex has conditions to appear. The complex never develops independently of other people, from the environment. If a person is accepted, if he is loved, if he is secure, if he has one to believe in, if he is needed, there is no room for the complex. Complexes are surmountable on the basis of healthy human relationships.

Alfred Adler creates a theory called "Individual Psychology" that affirms the understanding that each person has his own lifestyle and a final end goal that structures the style and the whole life. Neuroses, he says, do not come from our sexuality but come and have a reason in the lifestyle, that is, the lonely person is neurotic.

This particular feeling that guides our lives is the sense of power and superiority, understood as connection and acceptance by other people as a conquered individual value and significance. People are personalities who can compensate for their weaknesses. Alfred Adler met his death in 1937 during lectures.

The situational and the dispositional method of approach to the personality.

The Dispositional method of approach is a description of the personality through the traits or the so-called trait method theory. When talking about traits, we have to take into account several main points:

1. The trait should apply to all people.
2. How many traits to use?
3. What is a trait?
4. What gives/explains the trait?
5. Can we consider it as a cause of behaviour?
6. Does it always work?
7. Does the trait appear in every situation?

Gordon W. Allport

The idea of describing the personality through traits or dispositions comes from the American psychologist Gordon Allport (1897-1967). In 1937, he wrote a psychological book, and there he explained the traits as the main blocks of personality and protects individuality by saying that individuality is a unique combination of traits.

At this time (the 1930s) he does not explain that there are different traits. In 1961, Allport reviewed his point of view and introduced the details. Gordon Allport says that personality can be described by the conscious motivation, the mental health of the individual and the proactive behaviour, that is, the behaviour that comes from within that we produce and which is different from the reactive/stimulus response. Proactive behaviour is a projection of the internal action plans. Allport is the first theorist to work with healthy people. It must always be clear from where we bring the concept of personality - from inside or outside or from both. "The personality is what lies behind the concrete actions of the individual. It is essence, process, structure, change, product and growth. Personality is not just a mask and not just behaviour. Personality determines the unique adaptation to the environment." That is written in his book "Personality: A Psychological Interpretation". Even there he speaks of individual and common traits, but he does not distinguish them. The traits/dispositions describing personality patterns refer to the concept of "common traits", and the term "individual trait" refers to personal disposition. The common feature is a neuropsychic structure possessing the ability for equivalent behaviour and adaptation. Personal disposition is also a neuro-psychical structure, but it is not the same for all people.

Can we find enough traits which can be valid to describe the personality?

Hans Eysenck talks about 4 features:
1. Extraversion;
2. Introversion;
3. Psychoticism;
4. Neuroticism.

Raymond Bernard Cattell uses a test with 16 traits grouped into pairs.

Robert McCrae and Paul Costa create the Big Five model, they also use 5 main traits:
1. Extraversion;
2. Neuroticism;
3. Conscientiousness/consciousness;
4. Openness to experience/creativity;

5. Agreeableness.

The big problem of dispositional theories - critics of this theory affirm that behaviour varies greatly from situation to situation. There are situations in which a trait does not manifest itself and follows the question of whether we have this trait. But also the question of whether this trait defines behaviour and to what extent and whether the situations do not turn out to be stronger than the traits and have a higher value in determining the behaviour. Walter Mischel is a social psychologist and a critic of the dispositional approach. His studies show that the traits affect 10% of our behaviour. The point is that the situational approach if we assume it, obliges us to say that "personality is not a set of traits, but a dynamically structured system of traits and dispositions that are adequate to the situation." Kurt Lewin says that personality is a product of the situation and the personality's qualities to react. The relation between the behaviour and the situation is a personality's territory.

These models mark the fact that personality is the product of what is within and what comes from outside, and that reconciles many contradictions. The greatest chaos is around the concept of "personality"! Everyone declares what they are comfortable about.